Parrot Tales

8/01/22

For Bernardine
+ Bill,
Happy belated birthday
with Bill not far behind
Love,
Richard + Debby

Parrot Tales

Our Life with a Magical Bird

Debby Smith and Michael Steven Smith

with illustrations by Eric Hanson

OR Books
New York • London

Published by OR Books, New York and London
Visit our website at www.orbooks.com

All rights information: rights@orbooks.com

First printing 2022

Cataloging-in-Publication data is available from the Library of Congress.
A catalog record for this book is available from the British Library.

paperback ISBN 978-1-68219-378-5 • ebook ISBN 978-1-68219-379-2

"Human-tongued"
—Aristotle, *Historia Animalium*

For Eli

FOREWORD

Dr. Irene M. Pepperberg

I've known the Smiths and Charlie Parker for close to two decades. They hosted the party to celebrate twenty-five years of my research on Gray parrot intelligence and communication in their Battery Park apartment—with an appropriate Gray parrot cake, and Charlie acting as a stand-in for the famous Alex in our pictures. I've stayed with them or visited on several of my many trips to NYC over the years, most memorably after Alex had passed away and I was on a bittersweet book tour for *Alex & Me* in the autumn of 2008. Having Charlie wise-cracking during a phone interview definitely kept my spirits up! Thus, I was happy to accept when asked to write a foreword for their book about their life with Charlie. I felt that I had a pretty good handle on the task.

They asked me to write primarily about my experiences with Alex, but devoting the foreword to stories about Alex would be a disservice to Charlie, who is an endearing character in his own right. For me, the fun of being around Charlie is his spontaneity. Alex also performed a lot of spontaneous acts, but most of them were science-based and contextually appropriate. Alex would like to analyze a task, try to figure out where it was headed, and beat his humans to the punchline. For example: While we were teaching him to produce the sounds associated with letters—just as one does with children to teach them phonics—Alex jumped ahead and, when I was being slow in producing his favorite reward in front of a bunch of CEOs at the MIT Media Lab, famously belted out, "Wanna NUT . . . Nnnn . . . Uhhh . . . Tuh!" even though he had never been trained on the "u" sound. When describing Charlie's behavior, in contrast, spontaneity means that you never know what he is going to say, as can be seen from the tales in this book.

Living with—or even spending most of one's days, as I do—with a parrot is a unique experience. It's not at all like being with a cat or a dog. Dogs have shared their lives with humans for centuries, and enormous numbers of different breeds have been developed to fill whatever niche humans required—from hunters to shepherds to simple companions. We set up the rules and the dogs learn to follow these rules, generally by a human-designed system of reward and punishment. Our relationships with cats are not as strongly based on breeding, but the history is again long and complex, and we still exert a considerable amount of control over what is expected behavior. Our pet parrots, however, are at most two generations away from the wild—most come from wild-caught parents, and some of the older birds in captivity were actually wild-caught themselves. In nature, they live in large flocks, find a mate with whom they share their entire life, forage tens of miles each day—yet these wild creatures have, more or less successfully, adapted to sitting in our living rooms. They try their hardest to become "flock members" of their human family—to adjust to living with weird creatures incapable of flight, who refuse to even try to learn proper parrot communication signals. Instead, we insist that these wild creatures learn our signaling systems. In nature, parrots are prey for larger creatures, and without any logical reason, we expect them to trust us—individuals a hundred times their size—to provide food and shelter and safety. Anyone who has a parrot knows that you can't make a parrot do anything and retain that trust . . . you have to set things up so that the bird thinks that it wants to produce the behavior in question. You share your world with a creature that is in many ways as smart as a human six- or seven-year-old—but has the personality of a two-year-old stuck in the "no" stage forever . . . a creature that delights in outwitting you exactly because it knows that you underestimate its cleverness. You share your world with a creature that may be tame but is not at all domesticated, one whose quirks and talents frustrate and entertain you to the same extreme extent, often simultaneously. Pretty much anyone can own a cat or a dog; no one can really own a parrot—but for those willing to make a lot of accommodations, one can enter into an incredible partnership. Charlie's story is about that partnership.

I'll end this piece by noting that it was only after reading the book that I learned of how close I came never to knowing the Smiths and Charlie—maybe they thought that our mutual friend, Nancy Chambers, had told me of Michael's fatefully cancelled breakfast at the Word Trade Center on September 11th. I did know of Charlie's illnesses after the event, and how close we all came to losing him. I think of the turn of events like these and have to believe that such instances are not random . . . although I'm not at all religious, I have a gut feeling about the good that is generated by such seemingly random 'saves' in our universe . . . and believe that this book is one of those goodies.

Dr. Irene M. Pepperberg, PhD
Research Associate, Harvard University
President, The Alex Foundation
Author of *Alex & Me* and *The Alex Studies*

Charlie, an African Gray parrot, became a part of our family in 1992. We hadn't intended to adopt a baby bird. Perhaps we should state that more strongly. We not only had no intentions of adopting a bird, we hadn't even thought of it. We found out about this unusual bird store in downtown Manhattan, near where we lived. It was called The Urban Bird. We decided it would be an interesting Sunday afternoon destination, like a visit to a zoo, and headed off with our ten-year-old son Eli to check it out.

The store was in a neighborhood called Tribeca, a transitioning area. Not too fancy yet. There was still a parking lot across the street, a few bodegas and a diner, and The Urban Bird in a small building with a glass storefront.

All of the baby parrots were standing on perches or sleeping in little cozy nests. No cages. Just young parrots, all kinds, sizes and colors: Green ones from South and Central America, white ones from Australia, blue-and-scarlet ones from Indonesia, and gray ones with red tails from central Africa. No birds were stolen from the wild. Just domestically hatched, adorable baby birds.

Charlie was featherless at the time, having just hatched a few days before. He was living above the store in the nursery with other new babies, all having to be fed every few hours around the clock.

The birds in the store were young, with one exception. An

older bird was living in a cage, hanging from the ceiling in the back of the store, commanding a view of all who entered. While Debby paused by the entrance to read a *New Yorker* article about this "only in New York" place, Eli and Michael walked in. The old bird spotted them. He was evidently not a happy bird. He had been abandoned when the two guys who owned him split up. He saw us and yelled out, "I've got a yeast infection!" "What?" said Eli, looking up first at the bird and then at Michael. Before he could answer, the bird shouted, "Fuck you!" Instantly Eli responded, "Dad, can we get a bird like that one?" And that was it, there and then we decided to buy a bird.

BRINGING HOME THE BIRD

We named our parrot Charlie Parker. Every weekday morning there was a wonderful jazz program on the Columbia University radio station, WKCR, hosted by Phil Schaap, a jazz maven to say the least. He knew everything about jazz, all the musicians, their recording sessions and gigs over the years, who played with whom and where. The show, called "Bird Flight" was dedicated to the music of Charlie Parker, and only Charlie Parker, the great American alto sax player. Parker was nicknamed "Bird." He originally was called "Yard Bird" because he loved chicken.

"Yard Bird" was shortened to Bird. Eli and Debby listened to that program every day on the way to school. When it came time to name our bird, Eli suggested we call him Bird. But then we decided most people wouldn't get the reference so we named him Charlie Parker, with love and reverence for a great musician.

Charlie was too little and fragile to bring home, so we left him at the store for about ten weeks, to be fed and cared for until he was fully feathered and eating regular food. When there is no parent bird, the babies are hand fed a mixture similar to what a parent would regurgitate into their little crops. This is done with a plastic syringe. There is a danger that the baby formula will be squirted into the trachea rather than the esophagus, hurting the baby bird. We were not trained or prepared to take that chance. We knew nothing about African Gray parrots or any parrot for that matter, and had an oversized gray cat at home. But, enchanted with our little bird, we felt we were up to the challenge, even if we didn't quite know what the challenge might be. The Urban Bird was not far from our law office. We went to visit Charlie every day at lunchtime to hold him and talk to him so he would get used to us. We purchased a beautiful big cage, toys, dishes, and food, and, when Charlie was ten weeks old, we brought him home. Nancy Chambers, the owner of The Urban Bird, had raised Charlie thus far. She turned him over to us, gave us final instructions on the care and feeding of our new charge, and has been our friend and bird counselor ever since.

Most African Grays are about a foot long and weigh about a pound. Their brains are about the size of a shelled walnut. Males and females are monomorphic, that is, they look alike. There are subtle differences, but the only way to make a definitive determination is with a DNA test. We never bothered to do it, although we think Charlie is a male. Eli says that if Charlie lays an egg we'll change his name to Charlotte.

Charlie quickly became a part of our family. He got used to our daily routines, including departures for work and school, and to our habits at home. When he was one year old he said his first word, "Hello." Not a strikingly original debut vocabulary-wise, but Charlie made up for it subsequently.

That first word was quickly followed by an extensive lexicon of curses, wisecracks, offers of food and instructions to "get a job," many of which will punctuate the story that follows. African Gray parrots are very smart. In adulthood they are said to have the mental capacity of a seven-year-old human, though their emotional development is considered to be that of a two-year-old. When he was young, Charlie went through the "terrible twos." He was hard to be with. He bit a lot, which can be very painful. He screeched. We even considered giving him away. But we stuck with him and he grew out of it.

Parrots bond with one mate for life. Since Charlie was an only bird he had to make do with us as his flock, and pick one of us as a mate. It was unclear at first who he would fall for. The issue was settled one day when Charlie, sitting on Michael's index finger, bent down and bit him hard. "You son-of-a-bitch," Michael exclaimed, and reflexively dropped the poor bird. Charlie never forgot it. He and Michael have long since patched things up, but at that point Charlie bonded with Debby. Ever since, he tries to feed her, presumably so she will lay a good egg. And when he is mad he still says "you son-of-a-bitch" in Michael's voice.

This may be a good time to point out that having a bird is like having a toddler who is learning to talk. You have to be careful of what you say. Anything emphatic might become a part of his repertoire. And if Charlie really likes a phrase, be it serious or a joke, he will learn it and never forget it. As a teenager, Eli thought it would be funny to get Charlie saying, "I'm gonna kick your ass!" We have lived with the consequences of that teenage humor ever since.

Charlie has his habits and routines too. Once a day, in the afternoon, Charlie unburdens himself with every phrase and song he knows, going on and on until it could make you crazy or you leave the room. Sometimes in his rant he exclaims, "You're an animal!" Eli tries to divert him by whistling, clicking or making kissing noises, all sounds Charlie likes and will imitate and interact with. Sometimes this works, sometimes not.

Like all parrots, Charlie loves to play and make conversation with words or sounds. And he loves to shred wooden toys and scatter the debris. In the wild, many bird species eat fruit and scatter the seeds, helping the plants in their life cycle. Charlie throws his food. He's a messy eater whose surroundings are in constant need of custodial attention. Charlie has learned to command:

"Clean my cage. Sweep the floor."

Eli says that Charlie likes to self-affirm daily, saying, "What a good bird. What a gorgeous bird. What a fine bird. Charlie fine bird." Maybe we should all try this. Maybe we should have named him Charlie Feinbird?

Because Charlie lives in his big cage in our living room he is at the center of whatever is happening at home. He pays close attention to what we are doing. When Debby gets up in the morning and comes out of the bedroom to greet him he says "Hi, Dear," in Michael's voice. If Michael coughs, Charlie clears his throat. If Debby is tired and sits down, Charlie sighs. Michael is hard of hearing and Debby has a soft voice. Often when Debby says something Michael will say "What?" Now so does Charlie.

BIRD FEEDING

Charlie loves to eat. He has a hearty appetite and a broad but distinct palate. If he really likes what he is eating he'll pause mid-bite and say, "Is it good? It's delicious." He expects to be fed first and to get more if he says "want some" or "want some chicken," a word that horrifies strangers with its cannibalistic connotations but which we've come to understand is a generic term for whatever he happens to be eating.

Having said that, Charlie does love chicken, just like his namesake, Charlie "Bird" Parker.

Do you remember the old days, before online food ordering? When you dialed the restaurant on your landline and placed your order for delivery? One night, Charlie kept asking for chicken, again and again, but Debby was busy and not paying attention. Finally he decided he would take matters into his own claws. He imitated ordering by phone. First he made the dialing noise on the phone, "Beep, beep, beep, beep." Then answered it—"Hello!"—and then placed the order, "I want chicken," before giving out our phone number, correct to the digit. He seemed confident that in a half-hour the Chinese restaurant would deliver what he wanted, just as they did when we called. For a time, when we would get home late from work, Charlie would suggest, "Let's order out."

He has other food favorites. Charlie also makes requests for apples and water, and says, "Want some orange juice," which he will drink from a spoon. He also asks, "Want a beer?" He's never had that, but likes to be hospitable.

Passover is a favorite meal. He likes matzo balls and brisket, gefilte fish and chopped liver, and salad with dressing. He'll eat pizza and loves eggs, scrambled or over easy. It's fun to watch Charlie eat noodles. He grips them like a bouquet and pulls them up through his claw as he chomps with his beak. Birds like Charlie can't have chocolate, avocado, sugar, or drink coffee or alcohol. Otherwise he eats healthy stuff from our table. We even take a "doggie" bag home from restaurants for him.

ATTACK FROM THE SKY

In the 30 years we have lived together with Charlie we have shared many important life events. But while the current pandemic may yet eclipse it, none were more momentous and terrible than 9/11.

On the morning of 9/11, Michael was supposed to meet a friend for breakfast at Windows on the World, the restaurant on the top floor of One World Trade Center. They were to meet at eight o'clock. But his friend called to say something came up and he couldn't make it. It was the narrowest of escapes. We were still at home in our building, just across the West

Side Highway from the towers when the first crash shook our apartment. The reports were that a small plane had hit the World Trade Center. When it shook it again we thought we were being bombed. We actually saw the underbelly of the second plane from our living room window as it banked over the Hudson River and flew north past our building and into the second Tower. We went down to the street before the first Tower came down. If it had fallen over sideways it would have crushed us. But it came down on itself. We scrambled back to our apartment. The air filled with gray smoke, paper and particles, all swirling around our building. It looked like we were inside a tornado. We looked out the window but couldn't see a thing. It was literally dark as a mine. Then gradually it cleared. Everything was covered in a layer of thick white dust. Soon the second tower came down. A second blackout. We were lucky to be home so we could shut all the windows. It had been a beautiful September morning and many people had left their windows open before going to work. They came back to ruined apartments, inundated with toxic dust.

With Charlie and our big sixteen-pound cat Moe we weren't very portable, so we stayed put the first night. We were actually so freaked out we didn't know what to do or where to go. We tried to get our car but the parking garage door was electric and wouldn't work since the electrical generator was in Building Two of the World Trade Center. Everyone in our building left except for us and a blind bass player on the sixth floor.

The FBI rousted us the next morning demanding that we vacate, saying it was dangerous. There was also no electricity or water. We left large Moe for later retrieval, having been told an animal rescue van would be made available, packed up Charlie in his traveling cage, and headed up to the West Village, to the house of some friends who we had managed to reach by cell phone.

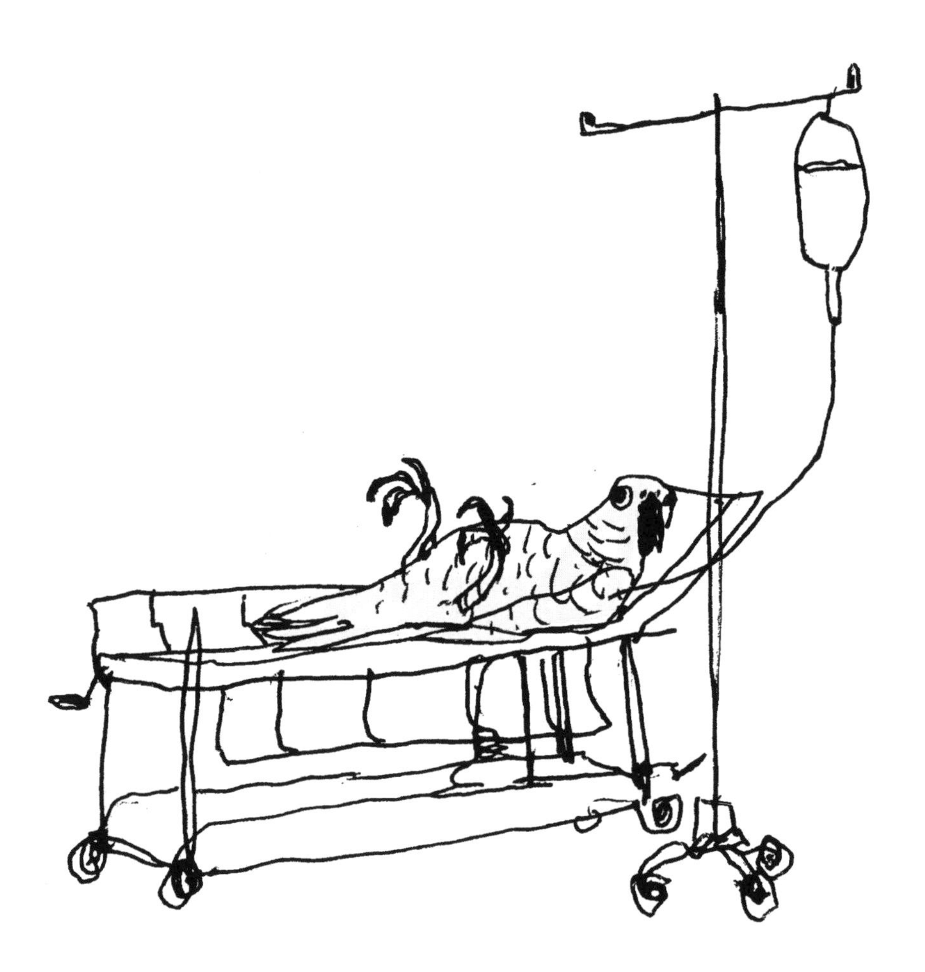

Everything was blanketed with a thick layer of toxic dust, the ash from the ruins of the buildings and their contents. We trudged north with Charlie swinging in his cage. "It's O.K. It's O.K." he assured everyone we encountered along the way. But it was not O.K. We almost lost him. Five weeks later Debby and Eli, now nine years older than when we first bought Charlie, and home for fall break from Oberlin College where he was a sophomore, noticed that Charlie kept closing his eyes and nodding out. He even fell off his perch. We rushed him to the Animal Medical Center on the Upper East Side where they have a specialist vet who cares for parrots. She checked out Charlie, put him on an IV, and said she was keeping him overnight. This was undoubtedly a serious situation. Parrots are very fragile. Because of their small size, high metabolism, lack of body fat, and efficient respiratory systems birds can die quickly when exposed to airborne toxins. Hence the canary in the mine shaft. By the next morning however he was evidently improved. When we called to ask how he was the doctor said she guessed he was feeling better because he had just bitten her assistant. She also said that the bill was going to in the region of $900. Michael replied, "But he was a victim of terrorism." At that the doctor said "Just a second," and disappeared off the phone. Returning a couple of minutes later, she informed us that she had consulted with her superior and that a fund had been set up for animal victims of terrorism and that there would be no charge. She gave Debby some antibiotics to administer and Charlie was nursed back to health. Moe the cat died of cancer three years later. Charlie still asks "Where's Moe?" and meows. Michael got cancer too. He was diagnosed in 2011, had radiation and two surgeries, and is now fine. We later learned that Christine Todd Whitman, the head of the Environmental Protection Agency, along with Rudy Giuliani, who fashioned himself as "America's Mayor," knew that the area was poisonous but misinformed the public, announcing that it was safe to return. Why? Because they wanted to get Wall Street up and running.

CHARLIE AT THE OFFICE

Our office was kitty-corner from where the World Trade Center used to be. After 9/11 we lost it for a year. Contamination. We could have found another office downtown, but we could not get phone service. So six weeks after 9/11 we moved all our files out of our office building and took them home. A big strong police officer from Staten Island with a tattoo on his arm and a flashlight in his hand helped us schlepp them from a darkened fourth-floor suite to our apartment several blocks away in Battery Park City at the other end of the World Trade Center ruins.

We practiced law right there in our living-room, with all our files stacked up near Charlie's cage. Running a business with Charlie as an office mate was a challenge. Every phone call was an opportunity for him to say "Hi, it's Mike Smith, how are ya?" Or recite our phone number over and over. One day Debby was on the phone with an insurance adjustor trying to settle a case. The guy was giving her a hard time. He was loud and rude. Charlie is protective of Debby. He heard the guy on the phone and was getting increasingly agitated, pacing back and forth on his perch. He couldn't stand it. Finally he yelled out, in Michael's tone of voice, real loud so the guy could hear him, "I'm gonna kick your ass, you son-of-a-bitch." The adjustor at the other end of the line said, "What did you say?" Debby told him she didn't think they had anything further to discuss and hung up, figuring any explanation would be implausible but was anyway unnecessary.

BIRD SONG

Get a job!
?

Charlie loves to sing. He has a deep repertoire, not of whole songs, but good chunks of them. He knows parts of the old rock 'n' roll number, "Get a Job . . . get a job." Our building's superintendent, Louis, a gentleman, was up in our place one morning fixing the radiator. He walked in and Charlie spotted him, saying, "Get a job, you son-of-a-bitch." Louis was both genuinely insulted and amused, and went around the building telling people about the Smith's bird. We felt bad about it. When we got home that night every neighbor we met said, "I hear Charlie called Louis a son-of-a-bitch!"

He also sings "You Are My Sunshine," a song written and made popular by a former governor of Louisiana who was also a country and western singer in the 1930s. It goes "You are my sunshine, my only sunshine, you make me happy when skies are gray." Sometimes Charlie telescopes phrases, truncating them. Hilda, who comes to clean on Tuesday mornings, is a big fan of Charlie's and he looks forward to her arrival, asking "Where's Hilda?" A religious person, she goes to Catholic church every morning before work.

Hilda comes in the apartment door, down the hall and into the living room. Charlie is sitting up high, on top of his cage. "Hola, Charlie," says Hilda. "Hola, Hilda," says Charlie. Perhaps Charlie is thinking of "You Are My Sunshine," when he then intones, "You are my son, my only son." Like the annunciation, but this time from a parrot. Hilda says Charlie is full of surprises.

Charlie knows he is a bird, and he likes the word "bird." He

You are my son! My only son!

uses it where he can. He taught himself to sing, "Charlie is a bird." Charlie also sings "Home on the Range" with Eli on the banjo, but he doesn't quite get it right. "Home, home on the range, where the antelope bird is heard." Then he trails off into a kind of whistle. He also does one bar of "I'm an Old Cow-hand." Michael tried to teach him "Istanbul was Constantinople," but he would break down into a paroxysm of guttural "ka ka ka" sounds every time he tried Constantinople. We were keen to teach Charlie "The Internationale" but he could not manage the hard K sound required for "'Tis the final Conflict." However, he redeemed himself by learning to whistle the song, out of tune like Michael, but still recognizable.

Debby thought it would be a good idea to teach Charlie a new song. We settled on "Down by the Riverside."

Gonna lay down my sword and shield,
Down by the riverside,
Gonna study war no more

Debby sang this to him endlessly. But to no avail. His only response was to yell out "WAR, WAR." So we abandoned the project.

Michael tried to teach Charlie the Bessie Smith song "Give Me a Pig Foot and a Bottle of Beer." Around that time, Eli brought a friend home from grade school. As they walked through the front door, Charlie unburdened himself with the only line in the whole song he had mastered, "Check all your razors, and your guns!"

Today, as both Michael and Debby are getting into the movies at the senior rate, Charlie on occasion reflects philosophically in song, "Enjoy yourself, it's later than you think."

BEING BIRD SAT

When we leave town and can't take Charlie with us, we bring him over to Nancy Chambers, our friend who used to own The Urban Bird. She is an excellent and passionate aviculturist, and, of course, because she nursed him along when he was featherless and just out of the egg, tells Charlie she is "Aunt Nancy." Charlie likes to go over to her apartment, which has a place set aside to board birds. We say to him, "Want to go see Aunt Nancy?" and he raises one foot. He's ready to go.

Charlie has a friend over there. Rusty. He's an African Gray, ten years younger than Charlie, and under Charlie's influence, if not wing. Charlie has taught Rusty some of his repertoire. When Nancy's phone rings, Rusty yells out, "Hi, it's Mike Smith, can you hear me?" in Michael's tone of voice. Like Charlie, he also says, "Tickle, tickle." Charlie raises one wing and commands, "Tickle my pits," but Rusty isn't there yet.

One night we drove back from somewhere and Debby retrieved Charlie at Nancy's apartment. Charlie and Debby took the long elevator ride down to the lobby, making frequent stops from Nancy's high floor. Charlie was in a friendly mood, secure in his small travel cage, saying "Hello" to people when they got on and "Goodbye" when they got off. But if that wasn't enough to cause a stir in the crowded elevator, the entrance of a dog started Charlie meowing, which he learned from Moe, the cat.

His mischief-making didn't stop there. When Debby got

off our elevator and carried him down the hall towards our apartment, she passed a young man who was delivering food from the local diner to a neighbor down the hall. Debby knew him because he delivered food to us too. As she was walking past him, Charlie, concealed in his little carrying cage, started making kissing noises. Debby apologized, saying it was the bird, but the man looked dubious.

CHARLIE HEADS UPSTATE

When Charlie was nine years old, we decided to buy an old farmhouse in the Catskill mountains, north of New York City. We had friends in the area and thought we would all enjoy having this funky little place where we could hike, bike, swim and have an organic vegetable garden. In the wake of 9/11 we were grateful that we had this haven to escape to for a while. Of course we brought Charlie with us, and he lives in the kitchen where there is a lot of action.

From his cage he can see if company has arrived. One of his

favorite guests is our friend Karen. When he sees her approaching the back door he starts to jump up and down and sings, "Get a job, dada dada." By the time she is in the kitchen they are both singing and jumping up and down.

Charlie is not allowed in restaurants. It is against the health code. But recently, on our way to the farm, we found a good Portuguese fish restaurant and a Jamaican one down the street both with tolerant owners who are not sticklers about the health code, and who look the other way when we bring in Charlie, in his little traveling cage. Charlie has so far been a good dinner guest as long as we share our meal with him.

Not to perpetuate a German stereotype of officiousness, but this relaxed attitude was not repeated when we took Charlie into a nearby mountain brauhaus roadside restaurant. We had him in his little carrier, under cover, and hoped he'd keep quiet. All went well at first. We were seated and we ordered.

Debby had Charlie in his carrier on her lap covered by the tablecloth. All of a sudden Charlie erupted, yelling out, "Where are you?" again and again. His voice was an exact copy of Michael's. People from all over the restaurant started looking over at our table. The manager came over to question Debby. She tried to explain that we were so hungry and it was too cold to leave the bird in the car. Because we had already ordered, he let us stay but he was not happy. "Don't come back if you have that bird." We never went there again.

CHARLIE ON THE CAMPAIGN TRAIL

Charlie appreciates company, and so do we, the more the merrier. So when we were asked by a friend who had been the head of the New York Civil Liberties Union and was running for Public Advocate if we would host a fundraiser for him we said we would be happy to. We just hoped Charlie would behave himself, as the speaker would be standing in front of his cage.

The evening arrived and we were ready: wine, cheese, standing room only for about sixty people in the living room of our apartment. It was packed. Charlie paced back and forth on his

perch, occasionally fluffing his feathers and jumping up and down. He was happy with the turnout. And so was our friend. It looked like a promising night.

Debby welcomed everyone, spoke of the importance of the Public Advocate office in a big city like New York, and hoped everyone would give generously. Now it was our friend's turn. He listed his past accomplishments and his qualifications for being the voters' choice. He explained his platform. He is a serious person and his delivery was, well, serious. With emphasis, he said he would make a very good Public Advocate. He paused. At that point Charlie said, sarcastically, "Sure." There were a few nervous laughs in the audience. The candidate went on to summarize his considerable qualifications for the job and ended up saying with great feeling, "I will make the best Public Advocate because I know what the people want!" Charlie, with equal feeling and emphasis, chimed in, "Want some chicken!" Our serious friend was not amused, "I didn't think I would be competing with a bird." Our guests howled with laughter and in fact are still talking about the night Charlie added his version of "a chicken in every pot" to a candidate's program. We raised some serious money for his campaign that night but our friend didn't win. He did, however, have a successful and meaningful legal career advocating for poor New Yorkers.

Charlie loves interaction and dialogue. Generally our guests are fascinated by him and greatly amused. They sing, talk and whistle to him. When Michael's cousin visited from Budapest, she sang "Somewhere Over the Rainbow" to him. He learned it with her accent . . . "Some vhere ohvair ze rainbow." Other friends are great singers and terrific whistlers. Unlike Michael, who can't keep a tune, they taught Charlie a melodious rendition of "The Internationale," and for the summer they stayed with us, Charlie whistled it perfectly.

CHARLIE'S ROUTINES

Every day has its predictable rhythm with our bird. When we get up and uncover his cage, he says, "Hi, dear," or "Want some orange juice?" After he is fed, he insists, "Wanna come up." We carry him around and share some of our breakfast. He loves fruit, toast, scrambled eggs, or a bit of blueberry muffin. If we are going out, he knows the signs. He starts saying with resignation, "Well, O.K., goodbye." Charlie has keen hearing, as well as eyesight and smell. He can hear people outside our door in the hallway. Our neighbors tell us that Charlie interacts with them while they wait for the

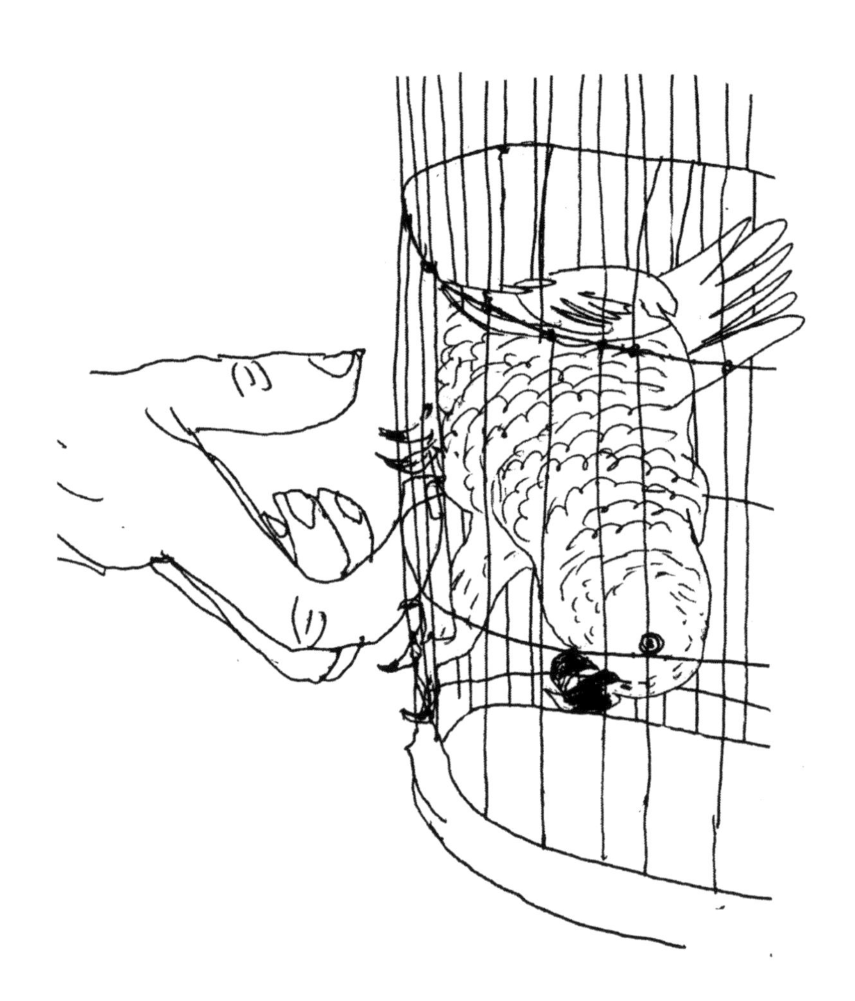

elevator by whistling, singing, or asking them if they want a beer.

Sometimes he'll take a bath, jumping in and out of his water dish like a Russian Kazotsky dancer. He soaks his feet and splashes water under his wings, and everywhere else. He really likes it.

Charlie looks forward to dinner and is an enthusiastic diner. We like to share meals with him, he so enjoys himself. Then the nightly cleaning and bedtime ritual begins.

When Charlie is tired at day's end he says, "Wanna go sleep." He will say it repeatedly if he has to. In fact, he'll also say "Wanna go sleep" during the day to get us to come over to his cage. But at night he gets weary. Grays sleep a lot—they are not night owls. So around nine thirty he'll command, "Wanna go sleep," and the routine starts. Then he'll say, "Want some water," so we change the water in his dish. He'll command,

"Sweep the floor" and "Clean my cage." Then he commands "Cover my cage," and then "Turn out the light." Before we cover his cage with a green cotton bedsheet, he hangs onto the side and demands, "Tickle my nose, tickle my toes, tickle tickoes." Sometimes he'll say, "Wanna mushky" (rhymes with push) which means a scratch on the head. So we'll tell him to "put your keppe (Yiddish for 'little head') down," which he does immediately and waits for the mushky. Other times he'll demand, "tickle my pits" and lift his wings so we can tickle him under his wings. When we put the sheet over his cage he asks, "Where are you?" We'll then raise the corner of the sheet, and he says, "Peek-a-boo."

The ritual ends at last with his saying "Night night" under the sheet. Charlie stands on one leg, puts his head under his wing, closes his eyes and sleeps. But if we stay up too late making noise in the living room, he'll command, "Eli, go to bed."

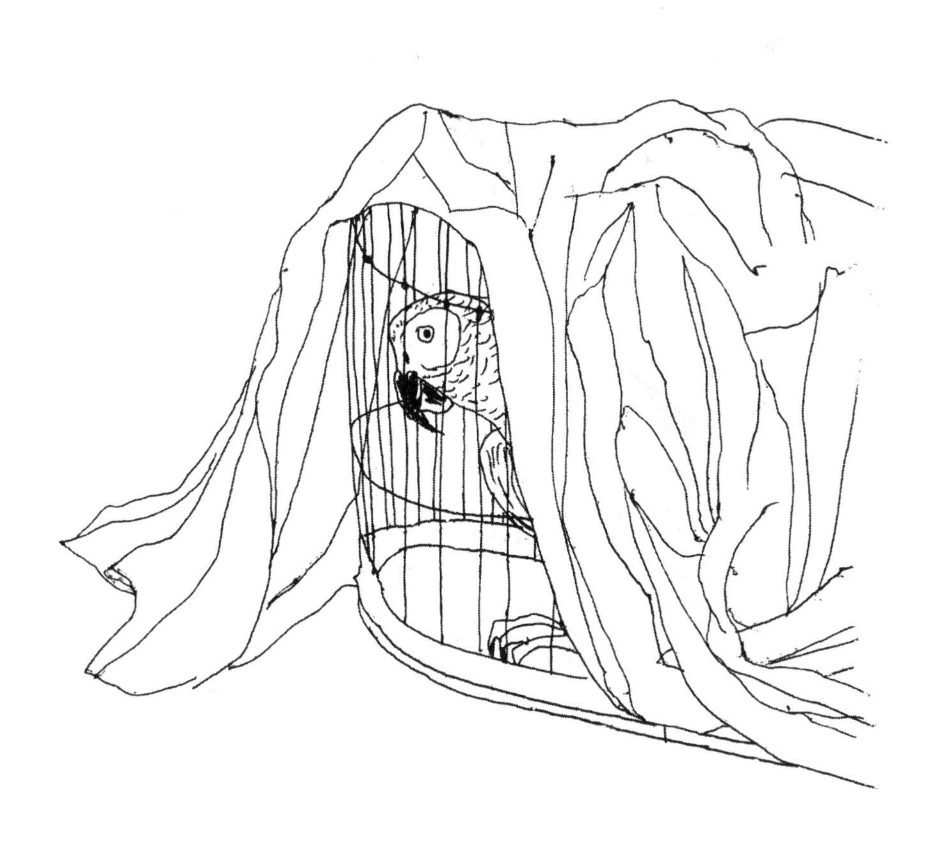

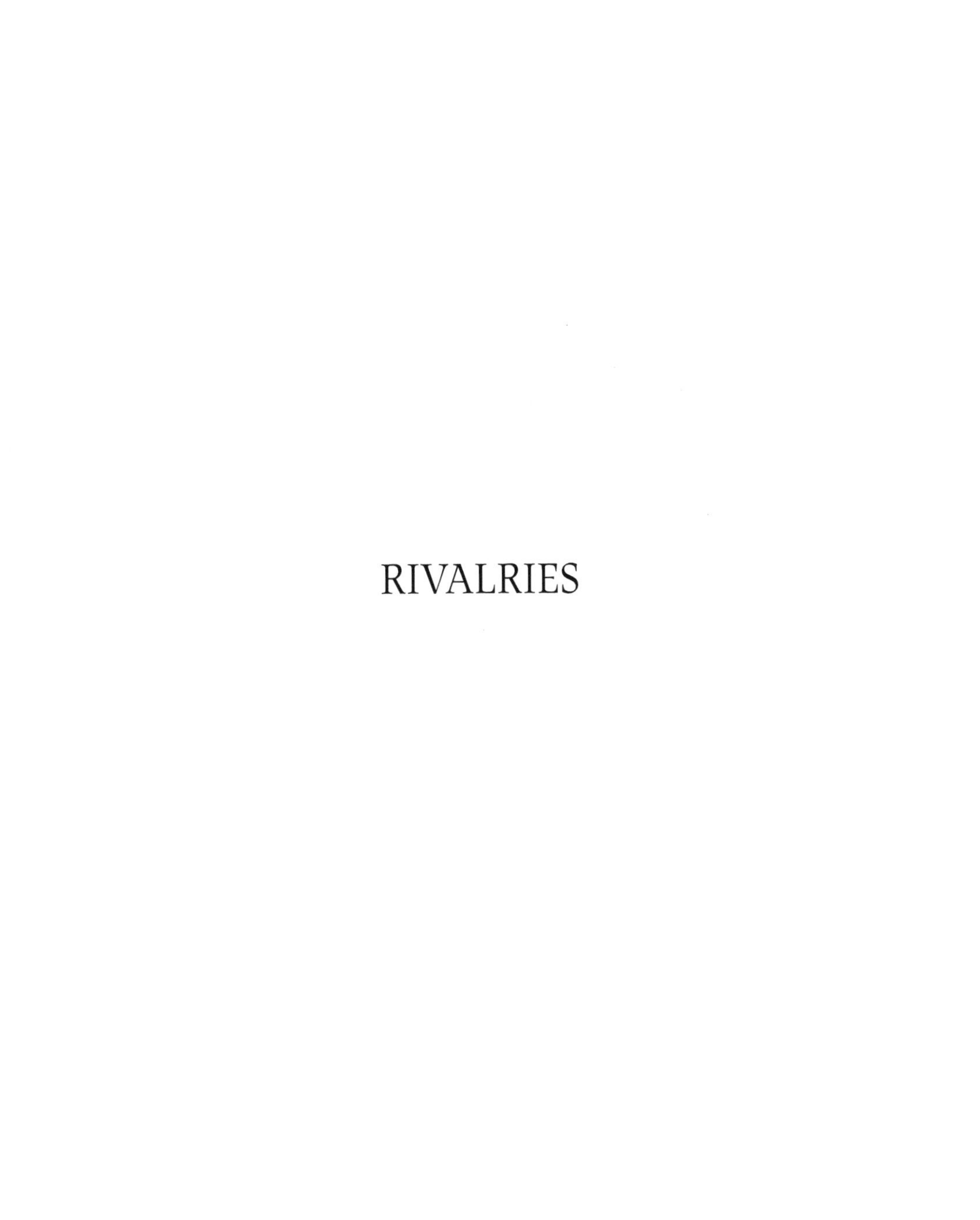

RIVALRIES

Every day is an adventure with Charlie. It is a bit like living with a small child. You have to pay attention and make sure they're ok, especially if there is another pet in the house.

Having a bird and a cat together may seem like not the best mix. But Moe was so lazy and self-absorbed that he didn't pay much attention to Charlie. He also wasn't the brightest bulb in the chandelier. Charlie seemed to know this and he teased Moe a lot. He'd whistle for Moe and say in Michael's tone of voice, "Come here Moe, come here," as though he had a treat for him. One morning Moe did go over to the cage and Charlie beaned him with a tasty bit of scrambled egg. Let's be honest, when he got the chance Charlie pooped on Moe too. But even Moe had his limits.

This was evident the day Debby saved Charlie's life. One morning we both were still in bed. Charlie had figured out a way to dismantle the lock on his cage and he got out. We could hear him outside of our bedroom door desperately pleading, "Wanna come up. Wanna come up!" Debby knew something was wrong. She jumped out of bed and ran across the room to the door, flung it open, and there was Charlie, one foot raised to come up, with Moe roused and ready, right behind him, about to pounce. Debby grabbed Charlie just in time and he got a new lease on his long life.

BIRD SMART

A story came out in the *Times* of London some years ago about Winston Churchill's parrot. It seems that after Churchill died the parrot was passed from person to person but the reporter was able to track it down. It was reputed to be 102 years old and still talked in Churchill's tone of voice, gruffly stating, "Fuck the Nazis." Churchill must have been very proud of his bird.

The world of parrot intelligence is no longer so unknown thanks to the studies of Dr. Irene Pepperberg and her coworkers at their lab at Harvard University. She has worked with many birds, but her longest and greatest collaboration was with an African Gray named Alex, short for Avian Learning Experiment. Pepperberg taught her bird Alex to identify shapes, colors, count up to six, add, subtract, identify objects, recognize and understand Arabic numerals, and, amazingly enough, grasp the concept of none. Alex understood the concepts of bigger and smaller, same and different. He did not just mimic or follow cues. Dr. Pepperberg's research with Alex proved that parrots are not mere mimics, that they use words appropriately: that they really know what they are saying.

Alex's level of comprehension was on a par with that of a chimpanzee or a dolphin. Irene demonstrated through experiments with Alex that, as she wrote in her book *Alex and Me*, animal minds are a great deal more like human minds than the vast majority of behavioral scientists believed.

Intelligence comes in endless forms. Animals use instinct, but they also think and feel. Common sense told us that but many scientists were opposed to the notion. Pepperberg wrote, "Alex taught me that we live in a world populated by thinking conscious creatures, not human thinking, not human consciousness, but not mindless automatons sleepwalking through their lives either." Bird brains are different structurally from humans. Bird and human brains diverged evolutionarily more than 300 million years ago. Birds don't have a cerebral cortex. They possess cognitive abilities despite having a brain that is non-human and non-mammal.

Alex was not only intelligent but possessed emotional depth. He could express thoughts about the world we shared with him. The last night he was with Irene, as she was locking up and leaving the lab he said, "I love you." He passed away later that night.

In contrast our bird Charlie, whom we don't spend a great

deal of time training , is just a member of the family and picks up what interests him. Sometimes it seems his verbal ramblings reflect a great deal of consideration. Like the day he announced thoughtfully, and all on his own, "Biting is ROICE." "Roice?" we thought. What is "roice?"

Then it came to us. He sometimes bites, and we say firmly, "No biting. Biting is wrong." We also tell him that he is a "nice bird." "What a nice bird you are!" and we pet him. What if he knows that biting is wrong but he wants to do it nevertheless, and gets a certain satisfaction from biting? Well then, biting is wrong but also nice—hence "roice," a combination of both his feelings and words. This is called a "lexical elision." Alex did the same thing by putting together "banana" and "cherry" coming up with "bannery." It was what he called an apple.

Parrots pass on their knowledge to younger birds, even when that knowledge comes from a human source or human society.

Birds across the globe, including starlings, warblers, finches, mocking birds and even the fawn-breasted bower bird of Papua New Guinea have begun mimicking human sounds, such as car alarms or construction noise, and teaching it to their young. In Dr. Pepperberg's lab, Alex would tell younger Grays to "talk better" when they mumbled their words.

Since Charlie has bonded most closely with Debby he covets her time and attention. If we have company and he sees others getting more of this than he thinks they should, he pulls the tried and true two-year-old approach. He squawks, then he whistles his most shrill annoying smoke alarm whistle. If she was too dense to realize he needed her attention surely she will understand it now, right?

Last fall Debby slipped and broke her hip and was taken to the hospital. Charlie was bereft and confused. Michael was here, but where was Debby? Debby had been photographing butterflies. Monarch butterflies for years flew north from Mexico to the Catskill mountains of New York where we have our little farm. But a terrible storm nearly wiped them out when it hit the valley in Mexico where they settle in millions over the winter. Their habitats are also being destroyed. Only recently have a few Monarchs returned to the Catskills. We grew milkweed for them to feed on, where the caterpillars spin their cocoons.

The caterpillars had emerged as butterflies from their chrysalises. Debby was thrilled and took photos of them in the backyard and then followed them around to the front, where she slipped on a walkway flag of slick bluestone, breaking her hip. She ended up in the hospital for six days.

Charlie kept asking for her. Then it came to Michael: Charlie needed to hear her voice. So Michael called the hospital on his cell phone, got Debby on the line, and put the phone inside

Charlie's cage. Charlie cocked his head and was soothed by her voice reassuring him that she would be home soon. He settled down.

We wanted to sell our apartment in Battery Park City, retire, take the money, and rent a place in Brooklyn near Eli. So we put it on the market. No takers. We lowered the price. Finally we got some interest. A young couple from South Africa who worked in finance and had two young children came to check it out. We were not allowed to be there for the showing but we heard the story from our real estate agent.

The couple walked in accompanied by their little girl. Charlie was in his cage in a corner of the living room. They came in the door, turned right, and walked down the hallway into the living room. Charlie said "Hello." The little girl approached the cage. Charlie looked down and asked, "Do you want a beer?" She was enchanted.

When they left, Charlie said, "Goodbye." They wound up buying the apartment. What a salesman!

We had to disappoint the little girl, advising that the bird did not come with the sale.

CHARLIE'S BIRTHDAY

April 10, 2017 was Charlie's twenty-fifth birthday. Why not have a big party to celebrate? Trump had just gotten elected. We felt we needed to do something silly, even ridiculous, to lighten our mood. So we did. We threw a birthday party for Charlie at the Jalopy Theatre in Red Hook, Brooklyn. Charlie was on stage, unfazed and unflappable, fluffing his feathers and happily bobbing up and down.

We organized the party with one of Charlie's most ardent fans. She had a commemorative birthday T-shirt designed

and produced with Charlie's photo on the front announcing, "Laid in Miami; Hatched in New York. April 10, 1992." And on the back, the motto "Birds of a Feather . . ." We distributed the T-shirts at the front door as people walked in to the theater.

Charlie loved being the center of attention. An adorable-three year-old unexpectedly sprang up on the stage next to Charlie and welcomed everyone. There were about seventy people there. Then a number of children came up on to the stage and circled Charlie, peering in to the cage. He remained unfazed, enjoying all the attention.

Next, Eli stood near Charlie and prompted him. Together they sang two of his favorite songs, "You Are My Sunshine" and "Home on the Range," with Eli on the banjo and Charlie singing his version, "Home on the range where the deer and the antelope bird is heard." It all ended with the traditional happy birthday song, Charlie's favorite number. He likes to sing,

"Happy birthday, bird!" We served an Italian three-colored cake, custom-decorated for the party with Charlie's name in birdseed, and we made a champagne toast: "Here's to Charlie!"

CHARLIE'S SPECIES

The common ancestor of parrots and humans lived in a different era of our planet in distant geologic time, some 300 million years ago. That's when our branches split. So to be able to talk meaningfully with Charlie across that great chasm is magical indeed.

Koko the gorilla died in 2018 at age 46. She was an icon for inter-species communication and empathy. She learned sign language and understood some 2,000 words in spoken English. She could easily keep up a conversation.

Irene Pepperberg's wonderful bird Alex died in 2007 at the premature age of 31. His amazing abilities became well-known across the globe. When he died, thousands of people wrote to Irene with expressions of solidarity for her loss, and theirs. It was extraordinary how Alex touched so many lives.

In the United States, Grays are one of the most popular species of bird pets. Across the planet parrots have been pets for more than 4,000 years, although they were never systematically bred like dogs or cats. There are images of pet parrots in Egyptian hieroglyphs. Noble Greek and Roman families had pet parrots. Alexander the Great had one 2,300 years ago. So did Henry VIII. Portuguese sailors liked their company on long voyages. In 1866, Edouard Manet painted one of his favorite models posing with a Gray parrot.

Devastation is being visited upon much of central Africa from east to west, where Grays come from. They are victims of limitless greed and desperation. The economic whip drives poachers in Nigeria. A wild African Gray can bring hundreds of dollars. Now there are very few Grays left in the country. Today, Grays retail in the US for at least $1,500.

It has been illegal to bring trapped wild parrots into the US since 1993, and it is also illegal under international law but they continue to be exported from Africa, Asia, and Latin America. One third of parrot species worldwide are endangered.

Wild fires raged in Australia, bringing a fiery end to 2019. Scientists estimated that over half a billion creatures were killed, including many Australian magpies. As the fires tore through the countryside the magpies were heard pitifully making the sounds of rescue vehicles, but to no avail. Their habitat went up in flames so powerful that the inferno could be seen from space. Humans have induced rapid climate change and we face the threat of a mass extinction of species, not seen since the end of the Cretaceous period 145 million years ago. At this critical time, we are intensely aware of our commonality and interconnectedness with other beings and with nature.

Cats, dogs and farm animals have been truly domesticated for more than 10,000 years. Human breeding has changed their behavior and morphology profoundly. Our life with Charlie has highlighted the interconnectedness we have with a nearly wild animal, in captivity for only a couple of generations, a descendant of dinosaurs, a non-mammal whose shelled-walnut-sized brain evolved separately from ours.

Humans since Aristotle have placed themselves on top of the animal hierarchy and apart from nature. We thought we were different and superior. This false belief has philosophical and ethical implications.

5780 on the Jewish calendar corresponds with 2020 on the

modern one. And of course 2020 was the height of the Covid pandemic. The enforced isolation, the lockdowns and the disease itself made life miserable. People were buying "pandemic puppies" for company. The counter men who slice the lox and serve the bagels at our local deli wear a T-shirt that proclaims "5780 sucked."

True enough. Charlie's companionship, his singing, his kibitzing and running commentary surely lightened things up for us. Who wouldn't be delighted by a one-pound, unflappable parrot strutting across the kitchen floor, belting out "Home On the Range" as loudly as he could.

Thirty years ago we had no idea we would be spending the rest of our lives with a parrot who in captivity can live a human lifespan. Two years ago, as 2020 began, we had no idea we would be plagued with Covid-19, and that we would spend the next couple of years isolated in our home with a sentient bird.

After thirty years of living with an African Gray parrot, and especially living with him over the last two, we better understand our role as stewards of nature and companions of our bird, Charlie.

For additional reading, we recommend:

Alex & Me and *The Alex Studies* by Dr. Irene Pepperberg

To fund Dr. Pepperberg's work, please visit

AlexFoundation.org.

All royalties from this book will be shared with the Alex Foundation with our thanks, love and respect for the work they do.

Debby Smith
Michael Steven Smith